Y.O.U.

Set A
High Standard
for
Being Human

By Bonnie Ross-Parker

Y.O.U.
Set A High Standard for Being Human

The Joy of Connecting
1231 Bickham Way
Smyrna, GA 30080
www.bonnierossparker.com

Cover Design: Diana Nichols
Book Design: Diana Nichols
Copyright 2004©

Lilli Publishing, LLC

For more information contact:
Bonnie Ross-Parker
www.bonnierossparker.com

ISBN: 0-9724061-5-8

Foreword

Life is a journey. Each of our lives is a reflection of the experiences we have, the people we meet, the thoughts we consider and the feelings we embrace.

Life is meant to be shared. No one chooses to travel life alone. Joy is in the shared journey. It's those opportunities we say "Yes" to, the people we meet or invite along the way, and the "ah ha" moments that awaken us to a new way of looking at something familiar. Our journeys continue day to day, as one experience follows another. The journey embraces people who impact us, circumstances and changes we can't control, the choices and decisions we make and the effect of those actions over time. The road is comprised of trial and error, risks and opportunities, pleasure and disappointment.

The word *"our"* lies within the word "journey". I wrote, *"Y.O.U. Set A High Standard for Being Human"* to strengthen the realization that our journey impacts others and the journey of others impacts our own. How we conduct ourselves and the value we place on our relationships determine the quality of our life. Consider embracing and implementing these standards with everyone and in every situation. I invite you to set an example of what is possible when we truly live our lives appreciating one another. Together, we can grow the global heart. It starts with *Y.O.U.*

Bonnie Ross-Parker
October, 2004

Table of Contents

Joy Of Connecting

"To me success means effectiveness in the world, that I am able to carry my ideas and values into the world—that I am able to change it in positive ways."

Maxine Hong Kingston

Deliberately Share Your Gifts With Others

"I encounter others to attend networking events."

Joy Of Connecting

All of us have gifts that we possess that can be shared over and over with others. What is your gift?

Think about what you have to offer and how you can share with someone. Sometimes just giving to others straight from your heart will inspire and enrich your own life.

Here are some ways that you can support others in their journey.

Be A Mentor

■ Volunteer at local organizations or community programs to mentor others in a skill or expertise that you possess.

■ Sign up in your local education system to support young people in the challenges of life or education.

- Check out your local university or college career programs for mentoring opportunities.

- Mentor a co-worker.

Request Permission To Offer Ideas And Suggestions

- At times you may be eager to share your observations or insight. Always get permission before sharing. You will find that when first you ask permission it will be viewed as a kind request and an opportunity to support someone.

- Simply say "May I share a suggestion?" Or "Are you interested in some observations?" Or "May I share my story with you about.?"

Share Experiences That Can Help Another's Journey

Tell your story. Everyone has a story. Many people believe their life is insignificant and pass up opportunities to share challenges and how they over came them. Tell a story of joy and success and lift up the spirit of others. Stories give people encouragement.

Provide Resources — Let Others Know About Your Best Contacts and Resources

■ When you find a good service refer it to others. That's one way to show your appreciation for valuable services rendered and provide support.

■ Maintain a list of the best web sites in your industry. Willingly share your database of business or networking opportunities.

■ Make a list of your favorite books and how they helped you.

■ Send newspaper or magazine articles to associates that might benefit from them.

■ Give testimonials on any seminar or workshop you attended and it's value.

What Five Steps Can You Take To Deliberately Share Your Gifts With Others?

Action Steps:

"Love from one being to another can only be that two solitudes come nearer, recognize and protect and comfort each other."

Han Suyin

Approach Meeting People As A Treasure Hunt

"I initiate conversation instead of waiting for someone to talk to me."

Did you ever play a game on the beach looking for the treasures that the vast ocean may have spilled on to the shore? Or perhaps buried deep in the sand you found a perfect shell or starfish. Remember the excitement you experienced? Did you find a treasure like a shark's tooth or a silver shell you didn't expect?

People are treasures in life. You don't know when you strike up a conversation with a stranger what treasure they may bring to you, too. Often, we pass up learning about someone because of the way they look, where they are from, or we're just to busy too stop and connect. You never know.

The person you take the time to learn about may be just the person to help you improve your business or life. Or most importantly, that person could become another friend.

Here are some ways to fill your life with the treasure of people.

Eliminate Judgment — Get Past Appearances

■ Criticism is a powerful energy and can impact your ability to be successful. Criticism is a form of resistance and can hold you back from developing rewarding and nurturing relationships with others. Become aware when you are judging people by the clothes they wear, the way they look, or how they talk.

■ At networking events or social functions introduce yourself to people who look as if they are there for the first time or seem to be uncomfortable.

■ Identify something to compliment a person on to start a conversation..

■ When you judge someone you are secretly saying to yourself "I am not confident so I must make myself be better than someone else to feel good." Make yourself aware when you start criticizing someone in your mind and change your behavior immediately to a positive thought.

■ When you take the time to see good things in others it makes you feel good and changes the energy around you.

Be Inquisitive — Ask Questions

Ask questions that inspire conversation. I know a man who used to ask people when he first met them what their passion was in life. He never had a dull conversation. Start with some of these questions:

■ What's your passion?

■ What makes you happy?

■ How did you meet your spouse, best friend, or partner?

■ If you could be anyone in the world, who would you be and why?

■ What's your purpose in life? Hi, I'm Joe. You look like a fascinating person and I'd like to learn about you. People love to talk about themselves, give them the chance and listen attentively.

Expect To Meet Interesting Individuals — Look For Them

■ Seek out the most interesting person in the room when at social events. Remember—you always have something to offer that someone else can benefit from.

■ Strike up conversations while in airports, book-stores, restaurants, waiting in line, at networking events, hotels and many more places. The opportunities are unlimited.

■ Follow your intuition if you believe you are sup-posed to talk to someone – sometimes the universe has a way of putting people together – act on that intuition.

Work At Expanding Your Contact Base – Participate In Diverse Activities

■ Set a goal each week of the number of new people you want to meet.

■ Join a class.

■ Sign up to volunteer somewhere in your community. Being on a team that supports others can give you a sense of accomplishment and satisfaction. It is a way to build a positive energy field around you.

Be Open Minded To New Situations

■ Embrace new adventures or ideas. Ask yourself how you can learn something new when feeling uneasy or hesitant to participate in new adventures or activities.

■ Look at opportunities with a different perspective. Embrace new opportunities with a mindset that you were meant to receive new information or opportunities.

■ Do something your would not normally do – break your routine.

■ Involve yourself in things you desire. It only takes one step to move forward.

What Five Steps Can You Take To Approach Meeting People As A Treasure Hunt?

Action Steps:

Joy Of Connecting

"I was always looking outside myself for strength and confidence but it comes from within. It is there all the time."

Anna Freud

Verbalize A Compliment Or Encouragement

3

"I offer compliments freely"

How many times have you felt unsure or uncertain about something? Suddenly you go somewhere and someone gives you a compliment or a word of encouragement and immediately you feel better. A friend calls and you are able to share your feelings and suddenly you feel better.

It costs nothing to give people compliments and the end result is priceless. Better yet, when you feel less than confident why not spend the day complimenting others – you'll end the day feeling fulfilled and grateful. Spend time each day applying these actions.

Be Generous In Acknowledging Someone's Appearance

■ If you think someone looks especially healthy, energetic and has that glow – tell them.

■ Seek out people who may appear shy or withdrawn and compliment them in some way.

■ Pay attention if someone has changed their hair or clothing style or lost weight in a healthy way. Acknowledge them for their efforts or accomplishments.

Be Generous In Acknowledging Someone's Accomplishment

■ Always congratulate people when they receive a reward or recognition. Don't allow feelings of resentment or jealousy to creep into your mind. The more you acknowledge others, the more opportunities will come your way.

■ Express your admiration to people who achieve their goals. Be curious about how they achieved them and ask if they will share some of their techniques.

■ Ask others to share how it feels to be honored or recognized.

Express Faith In Others – Encourage Others

■ Tell People "You're on to something big!" Be happy for them.

■ Use Terms "Good for you" or "I am so excited for you!" You'll start feeling the excitement too, if you allow yourself to.

■ Say "What a great concept"

■ Incorporate phrases such as — "Do you know how powerful you are?" Or "You are going to be very successful and I want to be there to support you when you reach the top."

What Five Steps Can You Take To Verbalize A Compliment Or Encouragement?

Action Steps:

Joy Of Connecting

"Loneliness and the feeling of being unwanted is the most terrible poverty."
Mother Teresa

Take Time To Listen Beyond Hearing

4

"I listen to what others are saying"

Do you listen to others or are you thinking about what you are going to say as soon as the other person stops talking?

Be aware of how attentive you are to others when they are speaking, sharing a story or just making small talk.

Salespeople make more sales by listening to the client and understanding their wants and needs than by talking. Take the time to listen to others and hear what they are saying.

Practice Maintaining Eye Contact

■ Look at one eye at a time when listening to someone.

■ Don't let other distractions take your eyes off the person while they are speaking to you.

Give Your Full Attention

■ Acknowledge the other person's comments throughout the conversation.

■ Stay interested by asking questions.

■ If you are truly interested in the subject being discussed ask them to tell you more.

Give Feedback And Clarify What You Hear

■ Occasionally repeat what the other person said "Let me be sure I understand what you just said…"

■ If you don't understand something ask for clarity. Don't be shy about saying "Could you explain that?" Or, "I'm not sure I understand what you are saying."

Eliminate Distractions

■ Move to a quite place if you are in a noisy area. Don't have a conversation if you must shout.

■ Don't multi-task when someone is talking to you.

■ Turn off TV's, video games, computers, and music when talking.

What Five Steps Can You Take To Take Time To Listen Beyond Hearing?

Action Steps:

"Only you and I can help the sun rise each coming morning. If we don't, it may drench itself out in sorrow."

Joan Baez

Care Beyond Superficiality

5

"I focus my networking on building relationships"

Often, when learning to connect while starting up a new business, we think no one really cares about what happens or if success is attained.

People do care about others. You can be one of the individuals who truly finds joy in connecting by caring about people at the heart level. Its about going beyond networking – it's about caring.

Follow Up With Individuals You Know Who Are Going Through A Hard Time

■ Stay in touch with friends and business associates who have had setbacks or challenges.

■ Let them know you care.

Offer Support When Possible

■ Send an email letting others know you are thinking about them.

- Mail a card or letter filled with encouragement.

- Invite them out for coffee, lunch or dinner.

- Give them a book or tape that helped you stay positive during a challenge in your life.

- Invite them to an event that is entertaining or humorous.

- Send them inspirational or motivational music that you find energizing.

Be Open To Expressing Concerns Through Verbal Acknowledgement

- Ask if you can help in any way.

- Share similar situations you've experienced.

- Find ways to laugh together.

Be Generous With Your Time

- Offer to help problem solve as an advisor or mentor.

- Offer to be a sounding board for ideas and solutions.

- Help others during their start-up phase.

- Recommend your favorite books.

What Five Steps Can You Take To Care Beyond Superficiality?

Action Steps:

Joy Of Connecting

"Follow your instincts. That's where true wisdom manifests itself."

Oprah Winfrey

Be Conscious About Being Conscientious

"I concentrate on creating my life as it unfolds."

The best time to nurture the brain to be fully present about your goals and opportunities is in the morning before the day's activities. Take time to consciously decide what you want to accomplish and how you and others will benefit from your efforts.

Think about what it's like to be "in the moment" and set forth a plan to stay present throughout your activities and interactions.

Live Life By Design

If you don't plan your life someone else will. Stay in control about what you want and design your life to reflect your desires.

Do Not Assume Anything

■ The time you assume is the time you will lose clear communication.

■ Always confirm and foster clear communications with friends, family, and associates.

■ Put agreements or plans in writing.

■ Keep asking questions until you are clear.

Ask Questions When Confused

There is an old saying "The only stupid question is the one you did not ask." Be willing to ask questions if you don't understand.

Focus On The Task At Hand

■ Remember – what you focus on expands.

■ If focus is difficult, post notes around your living or working environment that inspire you or remind you of your goal.

■ Write down your plans and goals and review them frequently.

What Five Steps Can You Take To Be Conscious About Being Conscientious?

Action Steps:

Joy Of Connecting

"You can't give people pride, but you can provide the kind of understanding that makes people look to their inner strengths and find their own sense of pride."

Charleszetta Waddles

Make Connections Unconditionally

7

"Every time I meet someone I feel the joy of connecting"

Look At Every Encounter From The Point Of View Of "What Might Be Possible"

■ Don't discount anyone.

■ Check out if you are feeling resistant or stalled and step forward anyway.

■ Take risks. Sometimes you take a risk and something good happens. Sometimes you take a risk and something challenging happens. If you are not willing to ever take a risk, NOTHING happens.

Give Generously And Expect Nothing In Return

■ Give from your heart. Love cannot be bought or sold, only shared.

■ Learn to let go of agendas and expectations of others. Honor others for who they are.

■ Pass on things you don't use or need to others.

Discover the Pleasure of Meeting New People

■ Set a goal to meet the kind of people you would like to surround yourself with and brainstorm ways to meet them.

■ Imagine the kind of friends you would like and what kind of conversations you will have with them when you first meet.

Exhibit An Open Heart and Open Mind

■ Be kind.

■ Be honest.

■ Refrain from talking negatively about others.

■ Be fair.

What Five Steps Can You Take To Make Connections Unconditionally?

Action Steps:

"I have met brave women who are exploring the outer edge of human possibility, with no history to guide them, and with a courage to make themselves vulnerable that I find moving beyond words."

Gloria Steinem

Celebrate The Success Of Others

8

"I feel excited when applauding wonderful news."

Successful people make decisions quickly and move confidently. They trust their instincts and remember how they created their success. Most of all they celebrate their own success and the success of others. Success does not come with all work and no play. Celebrating is the best way to feel good about your accomplishments. Share friendship with friends, business associates and family.

Believe In Abundance

■ Have faith in your abilities – Don't give up.

■ Defy the Odds – the most successful people have been met with challenges and nay-sayers and their defining success came when they realized they could defy the odds and did.

Surround Yourself With Successful People

■ Choose successful and caring people as your friends. Spend time with individuals who support and energize you. It is often said that your life is defined by the sum total of the five people with whom you spend 75% of your time.

■ Don't let anyone criticize your dreams and visions.

■ Listen to empowering tapes and programs. Hang out with people who do.

Praise Others Who Are Successful

■ Acknowledge others for their success – learn from successful people. Send a note or make a phone call to express your support.

■ Be happy for others who become successful – share in the universal energy of abundance.

Be A Cheerleader

■ Connect with successful people and ask what you can do to support their efforts.

■ Share their story of success with others.

■ Pass on good news — always focus on the good events in others' lives.

What Five Steps Can You Take To Celebrate The Success Of Others?

Action Steps:

Joy Of Connecting

*"There is only hope if people will begin to
awaken that spiritual part of themselves—
that heartfelt acknowledgement that we are
the caretakers of life on this planet."*

Brooke Medicine Eagle

Focus On Appreciation As A Way Of Life

"I appreciate all things I have I my life"

A young man from Haiti who dreamed of coming to America tells stories that every day he focuses on the things he appreciates.

He is appreciative of clean floors and a bed to sleep in. He is grateful for warm clothes and more than one meal a day. He focuses on the things we take for granted.

Don't take life for granted. Appreciate what you have and know there exists unlimited abundance.

Continuously Remind Others Of The Value They Bring You

■ Make people feel valued by expressing how valuable they are to you.

■ Acknowledge people who have supported you in your business, career, or during personal challenges.

Practice Spirituality In All Encounters

- Listen to your inner knowledge and act upon it.

- Focus on coming from a loving place in everything you do.

- Believe in love.

- Believe in equality.

- Be grateful every day for what is yours.

Express Gratitude to Service Providers

Appreciate services and businesses that add to your life such as banks, the post office, grocery stores, gas stations, and many, many more. The services that are simply integral to our every day existence deserve gratitude. We all have different roles in the fabric of society. Make certain you appreciate those jobs on which you depend.

Acknowledge The "Small Stuff" And Prepare For The "Big Opportunities"

- Don't take anything for granted. Every step is a step toward success.

- See little steps as the path to your continuous journey towards self-fulfillment.

What Five Steps Can You Take To Focus On Appreciation As A Way Of Life?

Action Steps:

Joy Of Connecting

"*I am a little pencil in the hand of a writing God who is sending a love letter to the world.*"

Mother Teresa

Thank People With Words They Are Not Expecting

"I use words that inspire and nurture."

Words have a lasting affect on our lives and the lives around us. Words are powerful. Words can help you connect with powerful feelings and are the tool to express what you are thinking and feeling to others.

Words are the daily messages that support us in believing in our selves and in others. Choose your words carefully and use them to energize others.

Express In Words That Are Meaningful To You

- I appreciate you.

- I couldn't have made it without you.

- What a difference you make in my life.

- I value your support.

- You are terrific.

- Thank you for caring.

- I care about you.

- I apologize for disappointing you.

What Five Steps Can You Take To Thank People With Words They Are Not Expecting?

Action Steps:

Joy Of Connecting

"The only thing that makes one place more attractive to me than another is the quantity of heart I find in it."

Jane Welsh Carlyle

Honor People For What's In Their Hearts

"I look for what is positive in each and every person with whom I connect"

How many times have you met someone and immediately they began to tell you about their product or service. Did you become annoyed?

Take a moment and listen with intent. Ask questions. Allow them to share their story. They need a listener!

You may make a difference in their life just because you listened or cared. Be willing to give the value of your time.

Allow People To Be Authentic

Be willing to receive as well as give. Connecting at the heart level means giving and receiving. It's a cycle.

- Listen with intention.
- Practice giving and receiving.
- Ask questions.

Learn From Your Relationship Journey

Take time to consciously review your relationship skills.
Do you have lasting and fulfilling relationships with
friends, family and co-workers? What areas might need
improvement?

Practice good relationship habits with everyone. Believe
in people and trust them even when it's challenging.

Give Everyone Your Gift Of Faith In Them

- Believe in people.

- Trust in people even when it's hard.

Ask For The Highest Good To Be Demonstrated In Every Connection

- If you approach people with an attitude there is
reason for your connection, good will come forth.

- Know love does not always look like you think it
looks in a relationship.

- Look for the best of possibilities in every connec-
tion.

What Five Steps Can You Take To Honor People For What's In Their Hearts?

Action Steps:

Joy Of Connecting

"We all live with the objective of being happy; our lives are all different and yet the same."

Anne Frank

Design Your Life In Ways That Bring You Joy

"I feel joyful when I'm connecting and meeting new people."

Show Others You Love Them

■ Express love often.

■ Let your behavior reflect loving feelings.

■ Engage in positive & loving activities.

Surprise People In Unexpected Ways

■ Send flowers.

■ Mail notes of appreciation.

■ Introduce people you meet to people they need to know.

■ Introduce people you know to people they need to meet.

■ Extend invitations.

What Five Steps Can You Take To Design Your Life In Ways That Bring You Joy?

Action Steps:

Joy Of Connecting

"You cannot hope to build a better world without improving the individuals. To that end each of us must work for his own improvement, and at the same time share a general responsibility for all humanity, our particular duty being to aid those to whom we think we can be most useful."

Marie Curie

Take The Lead In Contributing To The Global Heart

"I connect from a loving heart place."

Consider Every Connection As Added Value

- Define your values and practice them daily.

- Connections can be momentary or last a lifetime.

- Volunteer.

- Set an example of how to connect effectively.

- Share resources with those who can benefit from what you have to offer even when not in a position to pay you. In other words, "Pay it forward".

Be Willing To Forgive

- Let go of grudges.

- Recognize we are all imperfect and human.

- Forgiveness frees you up to be more loving.

■ The only way you can "turn back the clock" is to make amends for your mistakes and move on.

■ Focus on people's positive qualities rather than on their limitations

What Five Steps Can You Take To Take The Lead In Contributing To The Global Heart?

Action Steps:

Joy Of Connecting

"One faces the future with one's past."

Pearl S. Buck

Create Our Future From Lessons Of The Past

"I can achieve anything I set my mind to."

Plan, Do, And Review

- Develop a personal action plan.

- Journal what you want to accomplish.

- Create a wish list.

- Set realistic deadlines.

- Learn from past experiences what to implement and what to avoid.

- Look to the future with faith and optimism.

Create Your Future In The Present

- Recognize in every moment you are creating your future

- Begin now!

- Your past need not stand in the way of your future. Let go of what was.

- Be responsible for your own happiness

Find Your Unique Self

- Be a student of personal development to learn more about yourself and your behavior.

- Ask friends for feedback on what they like about you and what they'd change "if they could" about you.

- Trust the process.

Nurture Yourself

- Take care of yourself first.

- Take a vacation.

- Take small breaks and do something nice for yourself.

- Enjoy a bubble bath.

- Go for a walk in a park, take a ride, hike in the mountains, or visit the ocean.

What Five Steps Can You Take To Create Our Future From Lessons Of The Past?

Action Steps:

Joy Of Connecting

"Light tomorrow with today."
Elizabeth Barrett Browning

Expand Our Reality
From Lessons Of Today

"I approach today with openness as to what is possible for me"

Stop, Look, And Listen

■ Be aware of what you already possess.

■ Pay attention to your attitude.

■ What you focus on expands.

■ Recognize what "trips you" before acting out and living with regret.

Be A Student

■ Always be learning.

■ Take classes, attend lectures, participate in workshops.

- Be open to fresh ideas and the perspectives of others.

- Be willing to explore new horizons.

Live In The Present

- Don't allow fear stand in your way.

- Be willing to gamble on yourself.

- Now is the only moment at hand.

- Visualize where you want to go.

- Ask for help when you need it.

What Five Steps Can You Take To Expand Your Reality Fom Lessons Of Today?

Action Steps:

Deliberately share your gifts with others

Approach meeting people as a treasure hunt

Verbalize a compliment or encouragement

Take time to listen beyond hearing

Care beyond superficiality

Be conscious about being conscientious

Make connections unconditionally

Celebrate the success of others

Focus on appreciation as a way of life

Thank people with words they are not expecting

Honor people for what's in their hearts

Design you life in ways that brings you joy

Take the lead in contributing to the global heart

Create our future from lessons of the past

Expand our reality from lessons of today

Additional Resources

16

Books

Walk In My Boots - The Joy of Connecting
by Bonnie Ross-Parker

Bonnie Ross-Parker unlocks the key to networking in her dynamic and inspiring book, *Walk In My Boots - The Joy of Connecting*. Journey with Bonnie as she shares insights, ideas, and stories of how connecting with ourselves, with others, and with the world creates lasting value. *Joy* exists when we support and honor each other and when we feel connected to those whose lives touch our own.

Build It Big: 101 Insider Secrets From Top Direct Selling Experts

Would you like a resource that offers practical, proven answers to you and your team's greatest business-building challenges? Could you use fresh ideas on where to find new customers, how to juggle family and business, and how to find your next superstar? *Build It Big* offers you these strategies and much, much more.

Audio

Personally Speaking: My View On Life As I Live It—Volumes I-IV

Bonnie Ross-Parker shares her view on life as she lives it. Each volume contains 14 inspirational essays designed to enhance your journey and provide you with actions you can implement to enrich your life.

E-Book

ABC's of Great Networking

Most people have some fear around networking. They are not sure what, how, or when to network. Bonnie Ross-Parker and her co-author, Dawn Billings, have taken the guess work out of networking in their easy to read and understand book that makes networking as simple as learning your ABC's. They have broken 26 great networking principles into easy to understand and implement ideas that can transform your business, as well as your life, in a very short period of time. Take the time to learn the ABC's of Great Networking and you, too, will discover that networking is joyful as well as prosperous. Each letter is a beautiful graphic. Simply load this unique book into your computer to experience a new way of connecting in both your personal and professional life.

Bonnie is available for keynotes and workshops...

www.bonnierossparker.com

Phil Parker

Kiss Yourself Hello! A Journey from a Life of Business to the Business of Life

He's been hired, fired, acquired, merged, purged, downsized, rightsized…but never capsized! As a result, this former CEO has some unexpected answers to many of life's challenges. Phil's book creates an environment that gives individuals an opportunity to evaluate where they are in their personal and professional lives and encourages them to take action to achieve the success they deserve.

The Gift of Perspective: Let My Hindsight Be Your Foresight

Phil is skilled in the area of self-survival and exploring possibilities in the face of adversity. Held up at gunpoint at a young age, unexpectedly ejected from a jet plane and serving his country as a Naval Officer, were his training ground for what laid ahead in his corporate career. These experiences and more gave Phil the gift of perspective.

Phil is available for keynotes and workshops…

www.philparker.com

Bonnie Ross-Parker
Speaker/Author
1231 Bickham Way
Smyrna GA 30080
770-333-9028
bootgirl@bonnierossparker.com
www.bonnierossparker.com

About Bonnie

Bonnie is a multi-dimensional businesswomen/entrepreneur with a background in education, franchise development, publishing, mentorship, network marketing, and community development. She combines vision with a unique set of skills. Formerly the Associate Publisher of *The Gazette Newspaper/Atlanta*, she focuses her energies on supporting women. Bonnie is a graduate of George Washington University and achieved a Master's Degree in Humanistic Studies from Marywood College, Scranton PA. She earned a Certification in Network Marketing at the University of Chicago and several of her articles on owning one's own business and entrepreneurship have appeared in publications including: *Wealth Building, Home Business Magazine, Business to Business* and *Entrepreneur's Business Start-Ups.*

In 2002 Bonnie received The Athena Award ~ an honor designed to acknowledge women of leadership in cities throughout the United States. Currently, she is on the Atlanta Advisory Board for the Women's Leadership Exchange ~ a New York based organization offering conferences in cities nationwide, a professional member of the National Speaker's Association and a featured speaker with the Direct Selling Women's Alliance. Bonnie is the author of **"Walk In My Boots"** ~ *The Joy of Connecting.* She shares life with her soul mate, Speaker/Author husband, Phil Parker. Frequently referred to as *"America's Connection Diva"*, Bonnie's four grandsons call her "Nana Boots".

Printed in the United States
32410LVS00002B/190-759